SEGUE

FACING LOSS AND LIFE WITH LOVE

RACHEL STEIN

EWE ROCK
PUBLISHING

SEGUE

FACING LOSS AND

LIFE WITH LOVE

Rachel Stein

Ewe Rock Publishing

New Jersey

EweRockPublishing.com

First Edition: March 2021

ISBN: 978-1-7363094-0-7

SEGUE

FACING LOSS AND

LIFE WITH LOVE

From Part One, Inventory

Nature is not something separate from us; it is us.

Same as the storms in each season serve a purpose, so too do our storms. We can be effectively moved, sustained, balanced, and warmed. True also is the potential for chaos, shutdown, and irreparable devastation. Life happens, sure, but we can direct quite a bit too. We can prepare ourselves to weather the storms and be a ready receptacle for the favors of life as they come our way.

There's an energy that unites us all. That energy is love. We are stronger together, although we can never be truly apart, but we can be in conflict, which makes us think we are.

Peace provides our Wholeness, and Love sustains our Oneness.

It's a little book with a lot to say.

About the Author
Rachel Stein

Sometimes, life was rough and Rachel Stein saw more disruptions, eruptions, and interruptions than graceful segues.

She has witnessed and known many worlds and ways of life. A life that could feel like emotional whiplash as she went from her modest beginning as a Midwest farm girl, to the far-flung U.S. military global travels, to the cloistered ultra-Orthodox Jewish culture, and now as a woman reflecting and still creating a world of her own.

Rachel Stein has learned a thing or two about segues and how to keep standing and gently go forth through loss and life.

Ms. Stein currently resides in New Jersey with her quirky little family and considers herself their live-in mom.

For more from Rachel Stein please visit:

BooksandSuchbyRachelStein.com

This is a work of creative non-fiction.

All of the events in this memoir are true to the best of the author's memory.

Some names and identifying features have been changed to protect the identity of certain parties.

The conversations and events all come from the author's recollections, and are retold in a way to evoke feeling and meaning of what was said and what happened.

The views expressed in this memoir are solely those of the author.

TABLE OF CONTENTS

PART ONE

INVENTORY
PROLOGUE

Part of the fun of reaching old age is the retrospection. I look with a different vision now than the eyes I had when I was living through the experiences in real time. If we are lucky, there are many good memories to warm our souls. If we are luckier still, we see the great lessons there to fire up our hearts and fuel us to keep going.

Life unfolds in a couple of ways. Life happens to us, and life is what we make it. Many will add there's an element of luck too. Call it luck or call it blessings, we can make sure we are there to greet good fortune and be a vessel to receive mystical abundance.

Four years ago, in 2016, I took active measures to work on my physical health, and I'm grateful to say it has reaped a harvest of goodness for me that is now extending into other realms of my life.

Looking back before then, my eyes see the segue of five years' time where I was transitioning from decades of distress and beginning a steady process of emotional healing.

While there are pivotal moments in life, most transitions take a considerable amount of time, with plenty of twists and turns. We find ourselves experiencing what looks like numerous setbacks, but they are instead examples of us honing our new life skills to a higher level of competency. As the saying goes, "Time takes time."

It's the nature of nature. A week is still seven days; a year continues to be made of fifty-two weeks. Every season has its own kind of storms.

The tornadoes of spring are quite an effective means of rapidly moving air from one part of the atmosphere to the other. The rainstorms of summer provide us with life-sustaining water. The hurricanes of late summer and autumn maintain the earth's balance of heat.

The snows of winter provide a white blanket for the ground

and hold in the heat. So, too does each seasonal storm hold the potential to wreak havoc and destruction and annihilation. That's life, that's nature. Nature is not something separate from us; it is us.

Same as the storms in each season serve a purpose, so too do our storms. We can be effectively moved, sustained, balanced, and warmed. True also is the potential for chaos, shutdown, and irreparable devastation. Life happens, sure, but we can direct quite a bit too. We can prepare ourselves to weather the storms and be a ready receptacle for the favors of life as they come our way.

There's an energy that unites us all. That energy is love. We are stronger together, although we can never be truly apart, but we can be in conflict, which makes us think we are.

Peace provides our Wholeness, and Love sustains our Oneness. Some of us are luckier than others, and I'm feeling pretty fortunate right now as I take stock and look back on a few of my storms.

CHAPTER ONE

JUNE 2011
FATHER'S DAY

I miss my dad.

It feels like I should call him as if he is only a phone call away.

That is not possible.

He is too far away.

He is also close by.

I have felt his presence with me all day.

We never made a big deal of Father's Day,

Must be the energy of others I am feeling.

Learned from the news, roughhousing with dads helps with

Developmental growth and self-regulation.

I remember roughhousing, and that was the best!

There is nothing I want to say,

or hear, or do.

Thankfully, we did all of that.

I just miss my dad.

CHAPTER TWO

APRIL 2013
FIRST GRADE DO-OVER

I don't want anyone to get the wrong idea about me back in my time as a six-year-old girl. For years I've been telling people, I punched a boy in the nose on my first day of school. I did have run-ins with boys, but mostly in an imaginary way. All those westerns and war movies I watched with my dad left an impression on me. I never really punched a boy in the nose.

There were three boys that crossed my path in the first grade—Billy, Philip, and Johnny—and only one got a bloody nose, and he wasn't even the one I hit.

On the first day of school, I was forced by the threat of

my dad's belt to get on the bus alone and ride to school. Given that woeful choice, I complied and got on the bus. I found a seat in the middle, nearer the back. I sat there, by myself, head down and crying. The two eighth-grade girls sitting behind me gave me a tissue and some reassurance, and I stoically rode out the trip as the only first grader on the bus that day.

In the classroom, I was scared and bewildered. In the back of the room was the only mom left, and she was hovering over her tall weeping son, Billy. Someone said he was repeating the first grade. That angered me to see someone, a boy, older, crying, and being consoled by his mother. As fate and the alphabetizing of last names would have it after his mother left, Billy was assigned the seat behind me and still, he continued to cry.

By this time, nerves frazzled, I *needed* him to stop crying. I demanded that he did. When he didn't, I turned around and hit him in the face. The teacher was on it and swooped over to us. Towering over us, she looked directly at me. She said, "Use your words." My words were choked up inside. I looked away from her, turned back around, and slumped over my desk. Fifty-something years later, my words come to me.

The teacher said something to comfort us both and walked to the front of the class and started us all on our day. She made me feel like I was her favorite; looking back, every kid in her class probably felt that way. She would channel my strength that year by pairing me with the weaker girls to help them with skills I was better at.

Philip was a short kid with a chip on his shoulder. One day he brought straight pins to school and put them in a toy medical syringe. He told me he was going to give me a shot at recess. I had all morning to think about that.

In the playground, he jumped on my back and tried to make me fall. Being taller and stronger gave me an advantage. I spun around, trying to get him off of me. I leaned forward, and he went flying over my shoulders and crashed to the ground. That was that. The teacher swooped over to us. She confiscated all the pins before anyone received any injection.

Johnny and I didn't really talk with each other. He sat on the other side of the room, and we rode different buses. One day, he wanted the swing I was on and worked hard at pushing me off. I jumped off and told him to stop. He had an idea to negotiate for the swing. He wanted to play chicken for it. I didn't know what that meant. Amazed at my ignorance, he explained. We would stand several feet apart, facing each other, and then run full speed toward the other. The one to move out of the way was the chicken, and the other the winner of the swing. A crowd gathered. Johnny ran at me full speed, and I stood my ground. He was shorter than me; his nose was even with my shoulder. And, that's where his nose made contact; on my shoulder. That's how I gave him a bloody nose; all over my new red sweater. The teacher was on it. She swooped over to us. Johnny went to the nurse, and I went back to swinging.

I have no regrets about Philip or Johnny, but I do have regrets about Billy.

Looking back, I would want to do things differently.

I would want to have empathy for another scared kid.

I would turn around and smile and say quietly, "Don't cry."

I would have held out my hand to him instead of raising it against him.

I would realize we are all scared or angry or sad.

Life is always dangerous and frightening.

It is also beautiful and good.

It is always life and death.

We must choose life.

We must choose the attitudes and actions that support life.

Kindness. Humility. Compassion. A smile. A helping hand.

That's all we can do.

By staying mindful, we can stand our ground *and* be kind to ourselves.

In our humility, we can see that someone bigger, wiser, and kinder is managing the playground.

In our mindfulness, we can remember, the only acceptable way to interact with others is with compassion because everyone else is also struggling with something.

CHAPTER THREE

DECEMBER 2013
UNDONE

Undone, that's what it feels like. Un-this. Un-that. Last night during our discussion, I felt unloved.

I was loved, and then I was becoming unloved.

My teenage daughter said I didn't know her anymore. Looking back on the evening, I see neither was true. I am loved. I know my daughter. We were simply out of sync. We both came into our talk with heavy and undisclosed burdens, making us unable to listen to the other. We each came in needing to be listened to.

What was undone was me. I wept for hours.

My thoughts became stuck as repeated hurtful words echoed in my mind. The negativity was so thick in my mind at times, unbearable. All I could do was cry them out. At one point, I was able to focus on what my daughter needed, and I reached out to her and loved her and the gap closed.

Other times fear and dread washed over me.

"I can't do this. I'm failing. All is lost."

I'm trying hard to regain my confidence, my happiness, and my creativity.

All I could think was, it's fake and contrived. Pretending to be happy takes so much energy.

When life's demands come rushing in and needing my energy, the positive starts to unravel because it is unanchored. Everything feels unreal.

I feel doomed.

Is it true that it's not true? When I'm happy, am I faking it?

Honestly, the positive is true; the happiness is true. It *is* weak. Weak is neither false nor true.

Then I remember how fragile I am.

I am more like a young and tender plant with an old and large root.

I am no match for harsh winds, floods, scorching heat, or invasive pests. I can become blown away, washed away, burned to a crisp, or eaten up. On the surface, it looks undone, but the root becomes dormant, absorbs nutrients from the soil underneath the surface and sends up more tender shoots, and tries again to grow. This continual do-over is depleting the soil.

How do I fertilize the soil?

I'm tired. I'm tired of being the young sprout, the old root, *and* the depleted soil.

That's where the *I can't* comes in.

I need rest, and my life demands I produce or die.

That's where the fear comes in.

How do I feed, grow, and tend to myself? I've never been good at interweaving, and I have a teenage daughter to raise and a private practice to establish. I have so much to be grateful for yet, I feel stretched out and thin. Everything feels like loss and pending doom, not bountiful. That feeling of loss is the tidal wave of emotion that floods over me and makes me feel like I am drowning. I can't think. I can't find what I need. I can only fearfully flail and bewilderedly seek the shore.

If I'm busy drowning, my daughter and my practice are

not being tended to. If my daughter sees me drowning, she is actually being harmed. I cannot hide tsunamis. The tsunamis are coming with increasing frequencies. They are coming about once a week.

I need more support or at least a better strategy.

I am tired.

I lie cold and bedraggled upon the shore.

The sun will come up and dry me, but it is a winter's sun and not so warm.

I am no longer fond of do-overs and wonder how many more I can endure.

I would rather be.

I want *to be,* and I'm not sure how.

I will look for the now and strive to be in it.

I am tired.

PART TWO

LOVE
PROLOGUE

Funny thing about love is while love can strengthen and bind; love is also fragile.

Think about it; hearts can be full of love and yet break, even stop when the pain is too much to bear.

We must guard love and keep its load to a minimum. We must also design our lives to have love weaving throughout all aspects. Love is the essence of Oneness in all we experience in life.

CHAPTER FOUR

SEPTEMBER 2014
THE BED-MAKING DANCE

Every woman has her own way that she likes her bed to be made.

Sheet seams facing to or away; sheets all the way up or turned partway down; pillows standing up or lying down, and don't forget the exact placement of the accessory pillows and props.

Years ago, a close friend of mine confided to me her frustration she felt on the mornings she would try to cajole her husband of decades into helping her make their bed. He would pull the often-used ploy of feigning ineptitude to be encouraged to leave the task solely to her. This came from a man, who in his youth, had been a commissioned officer in the United States Army and knew quite well how to make a bed. This particular man was no slouch and took pride in excelling in any of his undertakings.

It made me sad for her when she told me this.

It brought to mind when I was a little girl, and we would go down to Kentucky every summer to stay at my grandparents' sprawling farm in the Appalachian Mountains. A favorite memory I have is sleeping with my mom on the featherbed mattress in the wrought iron bed that had been hers, in her old room with doors leading to both the rest of the house and the front porch. There was a feeling of vulnerability in sleeping in unfamiliar surroundings. Windows open in the summertime with the screens allowing in the cool mountain air and sounds of wildlife close by in the woods. Country living with dirt roads and the absence of streetlights, moonlight obscured by the yard full of trees, made the room much darker than I was used to. My grandparents were sleeping in the next room, and Dad seemed happy to have the upstairs all to himself. Any reluctance I had to going to bed was soon dissolved as I sunk into the downy mattress with its cool and smooth sheets with homemade quilts atop us. As I snuggled next to Mom, sleep was upon me in minutes.

In the morning, we would make the bed together. It is so much easier when a bed is made together. Every task of fanning, positioning, and smoothing is cut in half; yet, the pleasure is doubled by the satisfying feeling of being a part of a union, much like dancing with a partner.

Visiting my best friend in Tampa lets me relive those memories. While not a featherbed, every part of the bed my daughter and I share is luxuriously soft and engulfing.

In the morning, my friend helps me make my bed, and then we go into her room and make her bed. I follow her lead in all the steps. It is important for all aspects of the task to meet all her specifications. I love watching her step back on a job well done and seeing that smile of satisfaction on her face. It's meaningful for me to be a part of the dance that gives her so much pleasure.

I recall seeing years ago, a TV talk show psychologist on an episode where he was reaching out to a husband in a troubled marriage. The man was exuberantly arguing for more control in decorating his home with his wife.

The doctor told him how strongly most women feel about being the one who furnishes their homes. The doctor showed pictures of the bedrooms he had shared throughout the years with his wife. He also shared several examples of his apparent masculinity: being active in contact sports, his style of clothing, the big car he drove, all individual expressions of himself. All the while, he made a point of his awareness of his wife's need to express herself. She especially enjoyed having free rein in decorating their home.

The doctor's pictures revealed a long history of feminine decor in the master bedroom, although more recently, his wife had incorporated more masculine lines and colors to accommodate her husband's preferences.

The doctor's point was, neither his masculinity nor personal expression was threatened by honoring his wife's need and desire for decorating directorship. The opposite, in fact, as both were lovingly expressing feelings of mutual love and respect.

What an important message for any man in a relationship with a woman.

Our beds play a key role in our lives. Ideally, we are physically restored nightly. Our beds, also, are where we can give and receive intimate gratification. Our beds are where we end and begin each day.

The bed-making dance is a definitive process that embodies relationship enhancement as an opportunity to express our deep feelings for one another.

The way we choose to close our beds in the morning is a revealing expression of our creativity. Who joins or does not join us in that activity is a revealing expression of ourselves and our relationships.

How lovingly the bed-making dance is performed together is as telling as the lovemaking dance in the bed.

CHAPTER FIVE

JANUARY 2014
MAKING LOVE

Dear Daughter,

You may be surprised to learn, I want you to make love.

Making love is having an intimate physical connection that transcends physicality and touches the fragile yet empowering concept of love. It achieves intimacy on a spiritual level. While the bodies are connected, the souls are intertwined.

No matter who we have sex with, the souls will always connect on some level. It would be impossible not to.

The goal is to have the richest spiritual experience possible.

We want that because our soul is the most treasured part of us. It is pure and holy and deserves to be protected, adored, and nurtured to the finest degree.

Because of the potential for life, the act of making love is our highest level of creativity. Yet, we only dictate the outcome in a limited capacity. It is the Infinite Source of Creation who has the final say-so of the results.

Creating another human being, as you know, takes DNA from the mother and the father and has countless possible variations. The child could pull from the best of each or the worst of each, or somewhere in between.

We should aim for the worst-case scenario being the best we can make it.

By that, I mean, take as a distinct possibility the finished result could well turn out to be the worst genetics from each parent.

We, as parents, owe the child the best possible selection of DNA we can supply. It's important to be as healthy as we can be; in body, in mind, and in the soul. To be less is to gamble on another's eternal future, and that is plainly wrong and unkind.

Of course, not every session of sexual intercourse results in a baby, but every session does create. It is taught by the mystics that every act of physical lovemaking by the biblical Avraham and Sarah that did not make a child went on to be the soul of a future *ger* [convert]. Being high-level souls enabled them to create such lofty beings. We being lesser souls, create lesser entities; but create we do.

We create memories and imprints of future thoughts and feelings that swirl around the Universe for time eternal.

We may not have sex that will result in a person we will raise, but every time we have sex, we create intensely strong energy that will stay with us for the rest of our lives.

It's been said that it's as if everyone we have sex with will forever have their arms around our necks with the metaphoric possibility of showing up later in bed with us.

With the energy having the potential to add to existing energy in the world, what do we want to add to the Universe?

That's why I want you to make love.

I want you to make love that will nurture you and imprint so strongly upon you that you envelope yourself with precious, gentle loving-kindness emanating from you and nourishing the Universe.

Each of us is responsible for our own actions; as we take responsibility for what we do, we are better for it. We must choose well the company we keep. Powerful emotional tendencies to connect with others, and the neural mechanisms in place to mimic others will make it hard to resist copying the actions of those around us.

It is best to be mindful of ourselves and whom we choose to allow in our company. While sex is the strongest creative force, we are continually creating. Every time we relate with others, we create.

Again, aim for the possibility of a worse case outcome to be the best you can contribute. We are continually programming ourselves internally and externally. As best you can, stay mindful of what you contribute to your thoughts, words, and actions, whether your own original or those you observe and accept from others. We want each to be worthy enough for our keeping and passing on to others. That's all you can do, and it is enough.

Guard well, guard always, the most valuable part of you, your soul.

Dress her well in the finest apparel.

What are the garments of the soul?

Thoughts, speech, and deeds.

While each can lead to the other, each is equal in importance. We can only imagine what lasting impression a single thought, word, or action can have in life. Guard them well. Each is a vehicle for what you are creating in this Universe.

So, please make love.

I want you to make love.

I want you to mindfully and continually create kindness and pleasure, compassion and joy, awe, and happiness.

While you may only get to make a baby a few times in your life if at all, you continually and constantly are making a parent. All our creative endeavors are like children to us; we owe them the advantage of us being our best.

Every thought, speech, and deed you have add to your maternal profile.

It is inevitable. You are feminine, maternal, and sensual.

It is your gift, so please make love.

I want you to make love.

Of course, when it comes to having sex, like most things, timing is everything.

It is important to wait for a good time, the right time. Listen to your inner wisdom; that voice is your soul. She will steer you well.

When done properly, people are the most beautiful of beings.

I want you to live a beautiful life.

I want the best for you.

The best of thoughts in your mind, the best of words from your mouth, and the best of actions you can perform.

I want you to have the best friends and to be the best friend.

I have, I do, and I will always want only the best for you.

With all my love,

Mother

PART THREE

DARKNESS AND LIGHT
PROLOGUE

Yes, one of the definitions of darkness is evil, but I have come to see the black and white dualism way of thinking is a false dichotomy. I find more agreement with the other definition as simply being the absence of light. Our lives literally begin and end in the darkness, and we take refuge and find restoration there regularly each day.

From my new perspective coming from a place of light, I appreciate my darkness as I look back upon it. We need both. We need balance. They each provide relief from the intensity of the other. They are partners more than they are enemies. Time with only light or time with only darkness would eventually end us.

Nowadays, I look more for harmony.

CHAPTER SIX

SEPTEMBER 2014
THE RIGHT TO END LIFE

The right to end life.

Is there such a thing?

I once thought so.

I was in high school when the hot topic was legalizing abortion. In English class, we debated the subject. I was staunchly pro-choice.

Several years later, as my life took its twists and turns, I found myself in college, after becoming a mother. In a science class discussion, I connected abortion to birth control and was soundly reprimanded by the professor.

She had opted for motherhood later in life and had found it barely possible for her to conceive her only child. The idea touched a sensitive spot, and she vehemently opposed the idea of expectant mothers electing to terminate their pregnancies.

Along with a similar liberal view, I supported the idea of a Living Will to ensure one's right to die.

With more life turns, I lived for decades in an ultra-Orthodox community and logged countless hours of personal study and numerous classes touting the Choose Life philosophy. It would be logical to assume I was brought over to the opposite point of view by conservative persuasion. Instead, it was my personal involvement with ending a life that has made me strongly question anyone's *right* to end life.

While married to my first husband, and while he was stationed, by way of the U.S. military, in Europe, shortly after our son's birth, he shared with me a friend's confidence.

He told me, my close friend, who was married to my husband's close friend, wanted me to accompany her to get an abortion.

While I was touched by her trust in me, I refused. I was too much in the afterglow of recently giving birth. I respected one's right to choose but could not at the time be any part of that. I respectfully declined.

My husband went with her. She did not tell her husband because it was not his baby. I was told the pregnancy was a result of an indiscretion with a ski instructor. Years later, after both our marriages ended in divorce, by way of someone's tossed out comment, I learned there was more to the story, and no ski instructor was involved.

My understanding of Jewish Torah Law is: While life is always encouraged, the mother has the right to choose to end her pregnancy. The mother's emotional health factors heavily in her decision. We are taught life begins when the shoulders of a live baby come out.

Based on that, I helped someone else go out of state to terminate a late-term pregnancy. Admittedly, we were both quite ignorant of what that process meant. Prior to going out of state, we had spent an entire day visiting several local abortion clinics—each one denying service, of course, due to local state laws.

What impressed upon me that day in the various clinics was the seemingly uncaring and emotional detachment of the usually relatively young mothers and their accompanying others, usually their boyfriends or their mothers—flipping through the office magazines and everyday chatter between them. Was that simply a way to cope?

A late-term abortion is especially repugnant, and I will spare you the details, not unlike how I spared myself by not truly internalizing the process and choosing instead to focus on the needs of the mother. Sadly, she seemed to be forever traumatized by her choice. Maybe, not in a typical way. Immediately afterward, she appeared to be quite cavalier. She ramped up her before and often used self-soothing activities of sexual promiscuity and substance abuse. Years later, she would have another abortion.

Later still, she would give birth to two children and be grateful for their C-section births because she had come to gruesomely perceive her vagina as a death canal.

Now I see the emotional well-being of any woman considering an abortion as a legitimate qualification and to be weighed in the balance of what life-long emotional health risks are at stake if she chooses that option.

But I'm getting ahead of myself.

Shortly after, maybe a couple of years later, my life went through intense transitions. My oldest was off to college while the marriage to my first husband, my high school sweetheart, ended in divorce. I went to work, and my youngest started high school. We had two cats and two dogs, but even that would change.

The youngest dog, the two-year-old golden retriever, my son's dog, died suddenly and mysteriously. An autopsy eliminated what didn't kill precious Chester but failed to show what did.

The oldest cat, the twelve-year-old, twenty-pound tabby with a habit to hunt at night didn't return one morning. That night, the younger cat, the last one to be out and see our Caesar, uncharacteristically snuggled close to me in my bed and screamed all night long.

Our family was shrinking.

I felt burdened like never before. As a single mother working outside the home, to fit everything into my day, I rose daily at 4:45 a.m. and ended my days between 11:00 p.m. and 1:00 a.m.

It was one of the busiest times of my life. I worked full time, and carpooled my son to soccer games. I prided myself on being an active soccer mom. There was also Boy Scouts, synagogue attendance and involvement, and budding active dating for both my son and me. I took up running and participating in monthly 5K races.

I was always looking for ways to streamline my tasks and responsibilities. I decluttered the house. I gave away dozens of beautiful, healthy houseplants because I wanted freedom from caring for them.

Our ten-year-old dog was quietly dying. He had large growths on his mouth and body. The vet, whom we'd had for years, said the treatment would be costly and probably wouldn't make too much of a difference at this point. He assured me putting him down would be more humane than letting nature take its course.

I clung to that.

I thought about it for several days and spent quality time with my loyal canine friend: choicest last meals, a warm, refreshing bath. Time was spent stroking, talking to, and feeling love toward him. We set a date, and I took him to the vet. He was a kind, soft-spoken religious Christian man who had finally, later in life, married the love of his life and was starting his family with her.

Grover was a solid, heavy mid-size dog. We had rescued him years ago. He had long blond wiry hair and looked like a small briard with a low-to-the-ground body structure of a basset hound.

We placed him on the metal examining table, with my arms wrapped lovingly around him. We looked into each other's eyes. I felt he was looking trustingly into mine.

The three of us in the room shared a long history together. We had gone through animal sickness and injuries together. We had also taken time to talk with one another and confide our personal and professional triumphs and defeats. Today, we were respectfully and lovingly going to share death.

The vet injected Grover. We waited. We waited some more. Grover grew tense, and the vet more so. The dosage did not do the job. The vet, with tears in his eyes and a trembling voice, apologized to me.

"Could we save him now?" I asked.

"No, not now. I'm so sorry. Excuse me; I need to go out of the room for more of the serum."

He left us there together.

Did Grover know what was happening?

The vet returned and repeated the process. Unbelievably, like a nightmare, you are aware you are having, the scene repeated. Grover wasn't passing, and now he wanted off the table.

I shut down into the most basic of reflexes. I couldn't think. I lost my peripheral vision. I couldn't speak. The table was holding me up as I clung to Grover as he clung to life.

The vet was beside himself. More apologies. He left the room. He returned. The process, for the third time, was repeated, and not quickly - but finally, Grover died.

He did not pass over a rainbow bridge. He did not go down. He did not go to sleep.

He died while struggling to hold on to every ounce of life.

I brought him home, and my son buried him in the backyard.

Just as I had freed myself of the houseplants, my son wanted no more of the last remaining pet, our six-year-old cat.

Fluffy had been the kitten we kept from the litter of my son's cat, Patton. Patton was the kitten we had misjudged as being a male. *He* had followed my son home one day. By following, I mean he was carried by my son. Sweet Patton, the one I couldn't afford to have spayed and had given away.

Understanding my son's need to be rid of painful reminders of losses, I started looking around for a home for Fluffy. One of my co-workers at the clerk's office wanted him. She was a hardworking mother of two school-aged daughters.

She was happily married. She and her husband had recently bought their first home. She was happily focused on building her life while mine was disintegrating.

Fluffy was beautiful and small for a male, a long-haired tabby. He was well behaved, loving, and healthy, except for being FIV-positive. This was something my vet said was of little consequence as he was only a carrier and lived a robust active life.

I cowardly left out that information. So desperate was I to free my son and me of the last reminder of what represented to me, our contrived lives. I was desperate, too, to place Fluffy in such a remarkably good home ready to receive and love him.

Life went on with more changes. The son aced high school. I married seemingly well. We all lived overseas briefly. A few years later, I revisited my best friend at the clerk's office and bumped into the clerk who had so happily adopted Fluffy. We started talking, and I expected to hear happy tales of her family life.

She started her story with how madly in love both daughters were with Fluffy and how happy he was with them— remarking on his sweet disposition and his gorgeous shiny coat of long hair.

The story took a tragic bent, although she relayed it using

euphemisms of higher purpose.

A year or more after receiving Fluffy, she took him to the vet for a routine visit and learned he was FIV-positive. It didn't occur to her to try and reach out to me. I had married and quit my job. Apparently, her vet was of the school of thought an FIV-positive cat, despite being happy and robust, was better off to be humanely put down.

I listened to her talk about how the three of them, she and her two daughters, lovingly accompanied Fluffy. She gave the typical meaningful-last-moments-together speech, the one I've heard all too often. She shed tears as she poignantly recalled the event.

I stood silently listening. I grew numb. I lost my peripheral vision and felt physically distressed as if I had taken a powerful blow to my gut.

I viciously wanted her to feel as much emotional pain as her tale was causing me. So, I shared how he had been FIV-positive for years. I told her how my vet, like many respected in the veterinary field, had a different perspective. I said I hadn't seen the need to tell her because I knew she and the girls loved Fluffy. I told her how I had entrusted him to her.

The color drained from her face. She went silent. I had succeeded.

"I'm sorry." She quietly said and slowly walked away.

Not too long ago, about five to seven years ago, I was volunteering at a local nursing home. I had started there by helping my son, a seminary student at the time. It was a community service act of kindness and outreach. When he moved away, I continued the visits alone for a while. After a few months, my friend graciously joined me.

We were visiting the Jewish residents in a non-Jewish facility, so the list of residents was small. We started with only five. Oddly, there were no new people added, and the population naturally and organically diminished except for one more unnatural and enabled loss of one of the dearest ladies.

Gittie was a diminutive spitfire of a woman. She had moved into the facility with her husband a couple of years before and had recently lost him to heart disease.

She had prided herself in her appearance. She was impeccably dressed with well-coiffed hairpieces, her makeup and manicures always perfect. She loved to laugh and visit with us. She was opinionated and not shy about speaking her mind. She was strong about not wanting to be a burden to anyone. She chose to stay in residence rather than live with her only daughter, who would stop by frequently on her way home from work. Because her sickness could sometimes be embarrassingly messy, she declined the invitation to her granddaughter's out-of-town engagement party.

She wasn't quiet about having a Living Will and having someone *pull the plug* if her life was losing quality or burdening anyone.

When we visited, we saved seeing her for last because it was a way to leave on an up note and be happy.

And then she got dramatically more ill. She was admitted to the hospital. She was experiencing kidney failure. We frequently visited her in the Intensive Care Unit. She was always alone. She kept a death grip on the room's corded telephone, just in case she received any calls. She didn't receive any calls during any of our visits.

Kidney failure is not pretty. The patient's body swells up and is a sickly hue of yellow. The swelling made tiny Gittie look unrecognizable. She looked like a human balloon. Her wig was off, revealing a sparse head of stringy white hair. She had on no makeup, her nail polish was gone. Before, the mirror had been her friend. She had always enjoyed gazing and seeing her well-put-together appearance. I looked around the room and was grateful to see no mirrors.

Her bravado about pulling the plug had changed to now wanting to be put on dialysis. She told me privately, and quite strongly, she did not want to die! She wanted to do anything necessary to keep herself alive.

The last time we visited her, two doctors came into the room and asked us to step out. We did, and with the open door, we could hear their conversation. They were encouraging her not to go on dialysis. It might cause a coma that could last for who knows how long. They had spoken with her family, and they were alright if she was ready to let go. The easy option was to stop the medication, and she would quietly and comfortably be gone before the next dosage would be due. They stressed strongly and repeatedly how it would be a gift to her family to not burden them any longer. The conversation volleyed back and forth a few times until she was too tired to continue. They wore her down, and she agreed with them and signed a release.

They quietly left.

We quietly returned and spent a brief time with her.

We never saw Gittie again.

The right to end life. The *right*? Is there such a thing?

As a result of my painful experiences, I now beg to differ, or at least re-examine.

Certainly, I want to have rights over my body and my

choices.

My experiences have made me more respectful of life and an advocate for a better quality of life for all. More options are patiently and compassionately offered when we are facing life-ending and life-altering decisions free of ulterior motives or pressure from others during our most vulnerable times.

Someone used to tell me, "Even a fly wants to live."

I think about that, and now I trap and release little house pests I used to quickly and mindlessly kill.

I also know, no one wants to suffer.

Perhaps, more emphasis on preventing and ending suffering is what is needed.

When our lives are filled with love and peace and joy, the option to end it will not be as attractive.

It's on all of us to do what we can to lovingly enhance our coexistence.

Less please about sides and more about Oneness filled with love.

CHAPTER SEVEN

SEPTEMBER 2014
EMBRACING THE DARK

For as long as I can remember, I've been afraid of the dark, especially indoors. By simply keeping on a light, I not only illuminated the darkness, but I also stifled my fear.

Believing in the righteousness represented by the light, leaving on a light all night made me feel safe and a bit smug. After all, isn't it better, as we say, to light a candle than curse the darkness?

Look up the word darkness, and one of the definitions is wickedness. Most of us cut our teeth on that definition; I was no exception. It's a widely accepted philosophy of darkness. Something to avoid or transform with light. That mindset has its useful purpose.

I started seeing my issue with being in the dark was, in truth, my fear. I started to realize gaining freedom from fear was more useful than escaping the dark.

I have suffered more pain and anguish in broad daylight than I ever had imagined in the darkest of night.

All along, I sought out security and safety, and that's still important. Now, I seek freedom from the fear of what lies in either the dark or light. I want freedom. I want to be unaffected by my surroundings. To be aware of and yet not affected is what would give me the true freedom I seek.

Freedom and awareness give me a calmness of mind to go about cleansing away harmful elements from the dark and the light—a much better way to achieve security and safety.

This time in my life is dedicated to clearing away clutter that has piled up in my home, in my mind, in my body, and in my relationships.

I want to live free. I want to know true freedom. I want to release the fears I have.

I realize, instead of trying to be free from the existence of darkness what I want is to live in true freedom of the fear of darkness.

I decided to embrace the dark. As the womb is dark, so too is the earth. It is where we plant the seeds. Nighttime also provides the necessary darkness we need for a more restorative sleep, something I've been depriving myself of for years with a nightlight.

I found myself looking forward to nighttime. I wanted to embrace it. I wanted to revisit the feeling of being in the womb and being nurtured while passively reaping all the benefits. I wanted to revisit feeling cared for and engulfed in a life-enhancing environment. Last night, with the light source remaining the same, I only adjusted my thoughts to seeing the light being out of place and invasive. I had a most peaceful night's sleep.

As I think about the story of Creation, "In the Beginning . . . darkness was on the face of the Deep…" I'm struck with the awareness, darkness is where it all begins. We are conceived in the darkness of the womb, outer space is dark, and the grave where we return is dark.

My personal spiritual advisor recently remarked she sees me at a point in my spiritual quest where it would be best to return to the Beginning. I did not have a personal definition of the Beginning; until now.

It is the darkness.

The darkness: where I have been afraid. I have been afraid of the dark. In the idea of *Oneness*, I am the dark. I have been afraid of myself, afraid of returning, afraid of beginning.

I've been jumping over the beginning.

I've been living most of my life in the middle. That has caused multiple collapses due to my life's weakened infrastructure, and in some cases, the lack of infrastructure.

I have married and parented before visiting my beginning and developing myself away from it.

The personal and collateral damage has been remarkable. On and on are the experiences where I was pushed or pulled into, well before I was ready.

I misunderstood the cause of the failures. Out of frustration, I would quit or try again after shining a more glaring light on the perceived obstacle. I skipped over any idea of seeing darkness as being useful, as a source of incubation, or being, as Thomas Fuller said, "...darkest hour . . . before the dawn." I missed seeing things as they are and for the good.

Darkness can be embraced and embellished. In countless ways, we can prepare the darkness for optimum incubation. A skillful gardener will cultivate the soil before planting. A woman who wants to conceive a child can adopt healthy lifestyle choices to enhance her uterus to receive and grow a fetus.

Much of the darkness is predictable or can be manipulated. Nighttime is forecasted to the minute. Sometimes we have darkness forced upon us; it can be a surprise or unplanned with no time to prepare. Even so, often the outcome is positive by the very nature of the nurturing attribute of darkness itself.

As I choose true freedom from my fear of darkness, I embrace it and welcome it. Darkness is necessary, and its cloak is a blanket of comfort I now cherish. This is a time for me to return to the Beginning, to the darkness. It is time for me to slough off the outgrown hulls and time to regenerate.

Light has gotten the attention and has been considered the only good because that is what we easily see. Light is good. There is good also, in the dark. It is less easy to see because of the humility of the Gift-Giver. The gifts provided by the dark are modestly hidden away. Darkness is where we are allowed to be passive as we receive and accept gifts of conception, incubation, and restoration.

Maybe, I feared the dark as it marks the end of the day. The cessation of visible activity can appear like death. Harvest time gives way to shorter days. The graves of the dead are deep in the darkness. But night has begun. New seeds are developed. Essentially life is eternal, whether through reincarnation, procreation, or legacies of actions, words, or ideas.

Life is eternal.

Beginnings have ceased to frighten me. They are but loving gifts to me. They come in modest predictability that holds boundless potential and possibilities.

I am grateful for the dark.

As I pause, as with the night, I realize dark, which has always preceded light, is necessary and good.

CHAPTER EIGHT

OCTOBER 2014
WHO SHINES YOUR SHOES?

"Who shines your shoes?" I asked Donald as he walked through the door.

Shoeshines happened to be on my mind, as my daughter and I had recently conditioned our new winter boots.

My question evoked a memory for Donald. As a movie buff of films from the Golden Age of Hollywood, he recalled immediately a musical number Fred Astaire had performed. A number called "A Shine on Your Shoes." We found it quickly enough on YouTube, and Donald got a kick seeing it.

The lyrics have a compelling point about shoeshines. It tells us the remedy for feeling sad.

When you feel as low

As the bottom of a well . . .

When there's a shine on your shoes

There's a melody in your heart.[1]

How true!

My teen daughter and I recently bought new boots, and a bit of online research showed although the leather was finished and ready to wear, putting some wax on first would be a fine idea for preservation and protection. She had purchased a care kit along with her boots, and an application of the balsam would work wonders on both our new pairs of boots.

We set aside a time one evening and gathered all the necessary equipment.

I covered the table with some old newspaper; we had extra rags, disposable gloves, the care kit contained a soft cloth, and the tin of balsam with an applicator sponge. We took turns and shared the sponge as we kept busy rubbing our boots with the rags.

This was not my first time to put wax on leather, but it was my daughter's first time. She did a great job. She was faster than me. Her boots have a different finish than mine, which made them look more attractive with wax on them. My boots are going to look dull and unassuming, no matter what.

The whole task, from start to finish, took about twenty minutes.

I enjoyed sharing time with my daughter, and we both had a satisfying sense of accomplishment, not to mention a feeling of assurance about our boots' future well-being.

It's been years since treating leather has been done in my home. Certainly, my daughter has never witnessed it.

Years ago, my son, now grown and out of the house with his own family, would routinely take care of his soccer boots. He softened them, kept them clean, protected, and conditioned. I remember he used mink oil.

I remember how important it was for him to maintain his soccer boots. As a boy, he loved soccer and played from the age of five. He started with a recreational team and moved on to club and high school teams. In the beginning, we did not invest in the finest boots. This was a cause of concern for him. The finer boot and the higher investment was seen by him as our validation of his skill and ability. He appreciated the boots and what they meant, and how they added to his performance. He took pride in them, and he took care of them.

He had learned about caring for shoes from his father. Even though at preschool age, when his father was caring for his army boots, the unavoidable presence of boot polishing left an indelible early memory.

His father, my ex, had joined the U.S. Army at the impressionable age of seventeen. The military truly made a man of him and imprinted lifelong valuable skills, with self-discipline being one of the strongest.

Forty years ago, the footwear of the American soldier was a pair of black leather combat boots. The standard-issue was two pairs, allowing for one pair always being ready. The more dedicated soldier invested in a third pair reserved in peak condition for reviews and inspections.

Shined army boots are powerful. They instill a sense of discipline, obedience, camaraderie, self-reliance, confidence, pride, and especially respect. Those traits are forceful and make an impact.

The man devoted himself to the task of his boots with a tendency toward obsession. His collected and surrounding items would include rags, boot polish, water instead of spit, and a cigarette lighter to soften and sometimes melt the polish. The shine on his boots was impeccable. There was little difference between daily boots and inspection boots, except the cost and quality of the boots. A perfect shine is a perfect shine.

He enjoyed caring for his boots, and he took pride in the finished results. Like any task he did, he put in at least 110% effort. The task of polishing took place in the living room. The energy, the man, and the boots filled more than the chair and the side table. They filled the house, enough to make a lifetime impression on a three-year-old boy.

I remember when we were first married; I tried my hand at shining my new husband's army boots. On the kitchen floor of our two-room apartment, I took an extraordinarily long time and made an equally extraordinary mess of the surroundings. I was more than a little embarrassed when the utility man came knocking and exclaimed at my efforts.

For reasons I have yet to understand, my ex was less than appreciative of that display of my endeavors. Was I being too masculine? Had I shamed him? Was the work too shoddy and failing to be up to his standard of excellence? Whatever the reason, that was the last time I did his boots.

Years ago, when we lived in Texas, I owned a pair of western boots. I was particularly proud of them, and I took care of them. Although I haven't worn them in decades and hurt now when I put them on, I still own them. Looking through old family photos, shortly after Dad died. I noticed the undeniable resemblance of the western boots Dad wore when he rode horses. I have no memory of him caring for them, though. Of course, my childhood was spent out from underfoot of my parents and being outdoors as much as humanly possible.

I like the feeling I have when my shoes look nice, as well as when I see nicely cared for shoes on others. When my shoes look nice, I feel good about myself. It starts a process from the ground up. Nice looking shoes require nice looking clothes and hair and well, you get the idea. When I see others with nice looking shoes, I feel they care about themselves, and it carries over to showing the respect they have for others.

Thank you, Donald, for sharing your memory.

The ditty is right.

"When there's a shine on your shoes / There's a melody in your heart."

PART FOUR

MY HEART IS OPENING
PROLOGUE

Considerable and constant conflict and emotional pain do something to us.

I became so highly aware and sensitive and defensive I lost myself. Like in most suffering people, I believe the malady becomes its own entity and begins to nudge away one's own identity.

After having gone through my most recent divorce, I was often asked what I considered the epitome of a rude question.

"Will you still consider yourself a part of the community?"

I always answered honestly with the short answer, "Yes." In my mind, I was thinking, *Currently, I barely consider myself a part of humanity*. I could feel myself closing off and away from people. It was as if my heart was closing.

I remember an actress about ten years earlier hawking her new jewelry design that was an open heart. She had chosen an open heart after going through her painful divorce. She wanted to be open to life and to love.

I was going to need something stronger than a necklace.

We rescued a kitten, Micah, with the intention he would be my daughter's cat. He became aggressive and too much for her to cope with. He was over a year old when we rescued another sweetheart of a cat for my daughter. Micah was so aggressive we were wondering how safe it was for us to keep him. He and I seemed to find each other. Every morning while I was on the sofa, drinking coffee and journaling, he was curled up close to me. Stroking him and holding him for long periods of time every day apparently was producing enough love hormones for both of us. I started to feel my heart opening up again. I began to feel love again. My capacity for loving was resurfacing, and I stopped questioning my humanity.

CHAPTER NINE

9 AUGUST 2016
THANKS TO MICAH

Our sweet Micah is two years old today!

We rescued him from the shelter when he was eight weeks old.

Originally he was to be my daughter's emotional support animal (ESA), but he has become mine. Out on his own at five and a half weeks old, to an overflowing shelter in South Jersey, to our nearby shelter, to the tender place in my heart where my animal -love dwells.

We were drawn to this bold and spirited little beauty who looks right at you, and who in the private get-acquainted room at the shelter, would come out bravely and go back into the crate as he pleased.

This included reaching out his little paw and pulling the wire door shut; thank you!

Like most young cats, he grew and changed into many emotional and mental stages. He's brilliant and is able to communicate with me in that bilingual species-to-species way, as many animals are capable of doing.

He can fetch a tiny object; he can open drawers and doors. He will go for the house keys when the door is locked, and he wants to go out!

He also became a frighteningly vicious animal that would have been unwise and dangerous to keep, especially after we brought in Benny, the quintessential love sponge and one of the sweetest cats ever!

Something had to be done. Most effective and needed continually are the plug-in pheromone diffusers and the homeopathic calming valerian drops added to his food daily.

Additionally, we adjusted and changed from judging him as aggressive to seeing him as that frightened little kitten out on his own much too soon. Instead of seeing him as the problem, we looked for the problem we could resolve.

That kind of intention has enhanced our bilingual species-to-species communication skills.

It has given me a gorgeous, intelligent, and affectionate feline that starts my day snuggling with me while I drink coffee and plan my day. One who is always near and requests several daily sessions of petting, when before over-touching had been intolerable for him.

Perched on the windowsill upstairs, he likes to wait and watch for me to return and pull my car into the drive. He rushes down the stairs to greet me at the door and stretches out luxuriously on the rug while I stroke his face and neck.

We have developed countless other connections and rituals of bonding. Our relationship, like each of us, changes and grows.

I like to believe that is why we are all here on this beautiful, wondrous planet. Nature, with all that is alive and growing, is wanting to connect and express Oneness.

Sometimes though, fear arises and presents as an obstacle, masked in violence and aggression.

Learning to truly communicate allows our instincts to guide us and develop wondrous relationships.

We need only to launch the endeavor with our purest intention, and the outcome is richly satisfying and divine.

PART FIVE

LOVED ONES
PROLOGUE

They are the ones who launch us, sustain us, ground us and reel us back to shore. You can't have too many, and most of us have only a few.

In my saddest of times, I thought myself unlovable. As my mind cleared, I realized unloved is different from unlovable. As my heart opened, I came to appreciate my loved ones all the more, seeing them as my treasures and knowing being someone's loved one is my honor.

As my life moves along, I see love as the energy necessary for a life worth living and as the energy that unites us.

We are taught to love others as ourselves. In the beginning, we think of the separation from others and might consider that to be magnanimous. Later, it dawns on us, loving others as ourselves means we must first love ourselves. Later still, the concept of Oneness starts to permeate, and we get to the conclusion Oneness and Love are interchangeable. At our essence, we are one; at our essence, we are love.

CHAPTER TEN

NOVEMBER 2016
GENTLE FAMILY

I have a mantra. It is *Go Forth.* It has special meaning to me. It comes from the part in the Holy Scriptures where the Jews are backed up to the sea, and the Egyptians are fast approaching.

There are four camps debating on what action is best to take.

Short answer, God says, "Go Forth…"

The other day, I added Gently. *Gently Go Forth.* My heart sang. The word gently, resonated with me.

I looked it up, as I often do when words pique something inside me. I enjoy researching their meaning, synonym, antonym, and etymology.

There were no surprises until I got to the origin.

From Merriam-Webster.com: "Middle English: *gentil*, from Anglo-French, from Latin *gentilis* of a *gens*, of one's family, from *gent-, gens gens,* nation; akin to Latin *gignere* to beget - more at *kin*.

First Known Use: 13th century."

It struck me that originally *gentle*, meaning kind, soft, and amiable, was associated with one's family.

It later became associated with families of high station. Think gentleman.

It suggests to me there was an erosion of the connection to gentle for many families.

What happened? How did it come to be seen only as families of status?

I had never thought of the word, gentle or gently, being synonymous with kin. One's family could be described as gentle, but I had not seen the words being somehow interchangeable in usage. That family could not only be gentle but originally is, in fact, gentle.

It makes sense.

Our bedrock of *gentle* begins with our beget.

My mind went to the Book of Genesis, or rather its meaning. The beginning, the origin. In Hebrew, it is *Bereshit,* also meaning 'in the beginning.' Judaism teaches beginnings must start with loving-kindness, or they will break.

The same, of course, is true for families. They must begin with gentleness, or the families and the people in them will break. It's also true, one's gentleness or loving-kindness must start with our original family to ensure having wholeness and integrity in all one's life. The evidence is monumental.

As a mother, I thought about how it is my job to prepare and protect my children by providing them with their quintessential formation of gentle, loving-kindness. So much so that family itself is gentle.

It is truly the essence of parenting that supersedes anything else we can think to do for our families.

I thought about how I could and should place *gently* before all I do. Keep *gen /gent* at the beginning.

How all of humanity is a family and that all my interactions with others could and should begin with gentleness. Make family and gentle interchangeable. See all people as family.

Today, I kept that in mind as I interacted with my teenage daughter. I asked myself if I was providing her with family / gentle? The awareness softened how I interacted with her.

I watched how she responded in turn with gentleness.

Throughout the day, whatever the action, I reminded myself of my mantra, *Gently, Go Forth*.

I walked through the room differently. I made the bed differently. I ate my food differently. My body relaxed, and my posture softened. Calm and patience swept over me.

Not everyone has had a gentle beginning; in that case, now is a good place to start and gently go forth and begin anew. It's only natural. It's our birthright. Somehow along the way, gentle and family stopped being synonymous for many. Today, we can lay claim to our heritage and by so doing, we can bestow our legacy of loving-kindness once more.

"It's never too late to be who you might have been." - George Eliot

CHAPTER ELEVEN

DECEMBER 2016
GAM ZU L'TOVAH

Gam zu l'tovah [this too is for the good].

The long term overwhelms of my life has left me fragile.

But I continue to grow in strength and resilience, and the strides themselves make me happy, for I have much to be grateful!

My life has been equal parts grief and gratitude.

By focusing on gratitude, I believe I can build an integrated self that can be called happy and enlarge the gratitude portion.

But I need to remember my pain and trials and be permitted to mourn them in order to gently go forth and reconnect with my everyday and ordinary.

I believe that is where I will reveal the Divine!

Every day my peace becomes more powerful.

At times the present fragility gives way to a flare-up, which is temporary and when acknowledged and tended to properly, mends and becomes stronger, and that gives me joy.

That joy boosts me and launches me into a present-day mindfulness of all that is good before me.

The more I uncover, the more I find it is all good, truly.

The more that happens, the easier it becomes for me to trust and feel safe and develop more happiness, pleasure, and joy.

I must not be dismayed and put off track by my necessary pangs of growth.

Although I cry out in physical pain, I can be, and I am, at peace internally.

I am striving to gently, although at times painfully, embrace my reality.

I am gently going forth in life.

Sometimes I must gently, and with an understanding and forgiving heart, pause when necessary to give myself rest on my journey.

I can't always see how fragile I am and that results in me overstretching and causing myself pain, both physically and emotionally.

It's a process.

Gam zu l'tovah...this too is for the good!

PART SIX

SYNOPSIS
PROLOGUE

This segue of my life covered nearly five years of personal growth and insights as I transitioned from long term private and emotional crises, as well as much visible chronic physical pain, to the welcoming shores of healing for both.

Looking back on my writings, I notice I began with my father and ended with my mother.

Grieving both. One who had died but remains always with me and the other who lives and never to be found.

Only through love can I survive the pain each represents.

Love for each of them and love for myself and love for it all. Love is the energy that brings it all together, and love is the balm that soothes all the aches of life.

CHAPTER TWELVE

DECEMBER 2016
ARE YOU MY MOTHER?

Are you my mother?

I'm looking for my mother.

I look for her everywhere and in everyone.

Newly deaf new mother.

Colicky baby.

Fear and crying, both mother and baby.

Breast milk that didn't come in enough.

Underweight little baby.

"I got my first hearing aid when you were born."

Are you my mother?

I'm looking for my mother.

I look for her everywhere and in everyone.

"It's too cold outside; you wait for me in the house while I go feed the chickens."

Scooting a chair to reach the top of the bureau.

Hearing aid cords are not extension cords that fit well into electrical outlets.

Sparks and smoke and a little hand burned.

"What happened! Where's the fire? There's no one here to drive us to the Hospital!

I'll doctor you!"

Mom's hands were shaking as she doctored my hand.

Little girl sitting on the couch alone and frightened and hurting and worrying she's in trouble.

Day in and day out.

Summer visit at Grandma's and exploring trunks in the attic.

Little girl finds Mom's doll.

Mom says, "Mommy, I don't want her to play with it; she's too young."

Grandma said, "It's okay."

Shattered porcelain face on the hardwood floor.

"You broke the only doll I ever had."

Are you my mother?

I'm looking for my mother.

I look for her everywhere and in everyone.

Reading and writing and coloring and television watching.

Cats and dogs and clouds and trees.

All to occupy me while Mom does her housework.

Kindergarten and a new baby to take my place.

Little baby brother pees in my face.

More deafness and a stronger hearing aid.

"I got my first hearing aid when you were born."

Are you my mother?

I'm looking for my mother.

I look for her everywhere and in everyone.

Daddy's little girl.

Riding along on the farm tractor.

Playing in the hayloft.

Truck rides together to the Farm Bureau.

Are you my mother?

I'm looking for my mother.

I look for her everywhere and in everyone.

I think I found her on Mickey Mouse Club in Annette Funicello.

Who looks a lot like Mom.

"Your hair is too thin and too straight."

Little girl's home hair-permanent to look like Annette.

To look like Mom, who looks like Elizabeth Taylor.

"Your nose is too little, too round.

Aunt Mandy and I would pinch it when you were a baby.

Guess that didn't work."

Year in and year out.

Good grades and obedience.

School's a breeze.

Brother number two.

More deafness and stronger hearing aid.

Doctor says, "No more babies."

"I got my first hearing aid when you were born."

Are you my mother?

I'm looking for my mother.

I'm looking for her everywhere and in everyone.

"Sit down, kids.

We are getting a divorce, kids.

I'm leaving kids.

You'll stay with Mom, kids."

Angry mom.

Frightened mom.

Sad mom.

Crying mom.

Are you my mother?

I'm looking for my mother.

I look for her everywhere and in everyone.

I think I found her in teenage boys.

Boys that lie.

Boys that tease.

Boys that hurt.

Misinformed ploy to prevent Dad getting custody, Mom called the cops.

I'm taken away.

Behind bars.

Juvenile court.

Are you my mother?

I'm looking for my mother.

I look for her everywhere and in everyone.

I think I found her in Cousin Grace.

She takes me in that summer.

Big undertaking.

Me sleepwalking-climbing out the bedroom window at night.

That summertime between parents.

Daddy's little girl.

Moving in with Dad and Jean.

Niagara Falls honeymoon with Dad and Jean.

New home.

New school.

New Boy.

Are you my mother?

I'm looking for my mother.

I look for her everywhere and in everyone.

New Boy.

All the time.

After school.

Every weekend.

Life planned together.

I think I found her in New Boy.

Forever and ever, until death do us part.

Years of estrangement from Mom.

After saying I do,

New Boy taken to meet Mom.

"Did you two know you are distant cousins?"

Are you my mother?

I'm looking for my mother.

I look for her everywhere and in everyone.

Jean is not my mother.

She is Dad's Great Love.

New bride married to new boy Army recruit.

Living with Mother-in-Law, C.L.

Waiting to join Husband on assignments.

C.L. is not my mother.

C.L. is my home.

She's who I miss when I'm away.

She's where I can breathe again when I return.

She's open doors, and favorite foods, and late-night talks, and warmth, and love.

She's not my mother.

She's my home.

Army life and overseas and Stateside and overseas and Stateside and discharge.

A *dog-ter* [dog daughter] and babies and motherhood and sewing clothes and keeping house.

Strife and pain and divorce and remarriage to New Boy and divorce again.

Far from home and far from all.

Are you my mother?

I'm looking for my mother.

I look for her everywhere and in everyone.

I think I found her.

In God, in religion.

Seeking and seeking and seeking.

Congregations and learning and conversions.

In a New Love.

Bouquets of flowers, walks in the woods.

Hours and hours.

New Love says his teenage daughter needs him.

New Love has a full plate.

New Love says, "You understand."

Are you my mother?

I'm looking for my mother.

I look for her everywhere and in everyone.

I think I found her.

In deeper meaning.

In deeper conviction.

In searching, in dating men.

Men who lie.

Men who tease.

Men who hurt.

In prayer.

In belief.

In hope.

In Remarkable Man.

Talented man, intellectual man, man with heart and soul.

A much older man.

Man with wealth and man with dreams.

Are you my mother?

I'm looking for my mother.

I'm looking for her everywhere and in everyone.

Remarkable Man courts me and weds me.

Remarkable Man adores me and adorns me.

Remarkable Man takes me and my dear son to the Holy Land.

Are you my mother?

I'm looking for my mother.

I'm looking for her everywhere and in everyone.

I think I found her in Israel. In my New People.

In *shiurim* [classes] in *Shabbos* [Sabbath] and *Yom Tovs* [Holidays] in *shuls* [synagogues].

And *Ha Eretz* [The Land] as old as time.

Remarkable Man is unhappy, and we move back to America.

We leave my dear son and *Eretz,* and we leave our dreams.

We find a dream house and commit ourselves to our congregation and to our community.

Year in and year out, and year in and year out, and year in and year out.

New Baby Girl.

Miracle baby.

The only baby for a now older Remarkable Man.

Remarkable Man is unhappy with himself, with his lack of fulfillment.

Dear Son moves back to America, and we all join together in a new place, far from all.

Too far.

Too much.

Too little.

Good marriages do not end in divorce.

Divorce.

Custody battle.

Heart break.

On the brink of madness.

Sorrow.

I'm Daddy's little girl.

On the phone every day with Dad.

Every morning after coffee.

In the early hours, way before anyone else would think to be up.

He's my touchstone.

He's not my mother.

He is me, in that he knows who I am and reminds me of who I am when I have forgotten.

When I am lost, he finds me and says, "Here you are."

He's the one who says,

"You can handle it.

Kiss the baby for me.

I love you too, sweetheart."

Dad starts to slip away.

We both know it.

Dad is gone.

I call Mom.

Mom says, "Oh well, everybody has to die sometime."

Year in and year out.

It's complicated.

Remarkable Man, and I try again.

Second marriage.

Baby Girl's *bat mitzvah* [coming of religious maturity].

Marriage Annulment.

It's complicated.

Are you my mother?

I'm looking for my mother.

I'm looking for her everywhere and in everyone.

Calls to Mom.

A long distance visit or two to Mom.

She falls.

Surgery.

Rehab.

Living alone.

First brother is still the favorite.

He should be.

He steps up, all the time.

More calls to Mom.

Trying to get inside her head.

Trying to find her.

She's had hard times.

She always, always worked hard.

She did her best, it was never easy.

She remembers every birthday.

Ten-dollar bill inside.

She remembers Chanukah too.

She doesn't call because she doesn't have a calling plan.

I seldom call her.

She's too far to go see.

She's too hard to reach.

She's my mother.

I found her everywhere and in everyone.

She's in the men I married.

She's in the religion I seek.

She's in every critical, judgmental person in my life.

She's in the corny jokes I tell.

She's in the mirror.

She's in my fears.

She's in my habits I love and the habits I hate.

She's in my collapses and my strengths.

She's in my words I write, and the books I read, and the prayers I say.

How is it, I don't know her or who she is?

How is it, she will never ever be able to truly hear me?

How is it, she doesn't know who I am?

Are you my mother?

I'm looking for my mother.

I look for her everywhere and in everyone.

I found her.

She is everywhere.

She is everyone.

Are you my mother?

I'm looking for my mother.

I look for her everywhere and in everyone.

I will never find her.

EPILOGUE

Mom died this year, in Springtime 2020, during the first peak of the Pandemic in America, but not from the virus.

She was in-home hospice for eighteen days, even though the prognosis had been for only two and, at best, three days.

She wasn't dying, but she died. She simply wore out from mistreatments and misjudgments.

The same could be said about her living.

Born with a slight hearing impairment made worse throughout her life as she experienced chronic sinus infections, she was always a bit out of sync with her environment.

Her last couple of years, she was even more so; concussions from falls and misaligned medications had affected her mind. She lost touch with reality, and I lost touch with her.

I didn't even know she had been in the hospital for three weeks before she came home to hospice.

We saw each other last, maybe eight years ago. I had driven two days over mountain peaks to spend a few days together. She was Mom with white hair. She could walk in Walmart. She bought a bikini for her granddaughter and a Bed Buddy heating pad for me for my birthday. Neither of us knew then where we each were in our life stages. I was in my chronic muscle pain time of life and would find ways to heal and get better. She was at the end of her prime and would spend years declining from accidents and surgeries and falls.

We would lose five mutual close family loved ones, but they left packed in brief succession during her time of confusion. I told her over the phone about the first one. She couldn't reconcile the information, and it jumbled with the deceased's father. She knew she was confused, likely from her medications needing adjustments. She asked me if her mother was dead. Granny had been gone for about thirty years. She said she knew that and still, she felt like she was still stuck in the past when Granny was alive. She knew her thoughts were distorted.

My brother and I agreed she would not be told any more news like that over the phone. Deaths would be reported when her mind was clear enough. The rest died without her ever knowing, which was just as well.

Some losses are too great and painful even for the best of us to bear.

The frequent phone calls became less so as she was in and out of hospitals and rehabs without the benefit of her caption telephone to read the calls.

The last couple of years at home, under loving family care, was her declining time.

Without visits or pictures, my visions of her stayed as she appeared when we were last together.

My last vision of her through a visual phone app was as one would expect someone almost ninety to look like in a hospice. I was not expecting it, and I was not emotionally prepared to see her like that.

Scraggly white hair, dark and sunken eyes closed, an oxygen tube in the nose, all shook me to my core.

Grief swept over me, and compassion, and love.

Overwhelm to make her, me, everything, better.

Dying literally reduces everything.

All the air goes out.

What's left is love.

Everything else is superfluous.

The several phone calls over her last days were of me verbalizing love and reassurance and what I intended as comfort.

At night, I put on a musical playlist of her favorites, and I imagined she, in a more-free spiritual form, was in my room with me, listening.

Miles and miles apart, without the phone, I had deeper, more personal conversations with her, and I felt her listening.

Now, for the first time in my life, as she lay dying, I felt she could hear me.

All obstacles were gone as we communed heart to heart and soul to soul.

Some days, there seemed hope for a rally and recovery, but she was too weak to recover all that had been thrust upon her aging body. She wasn't dying, but she gave out and died.

Her last night on Earth, I dreamed of her, and she told me she was confused and looking for her directions on where to go next.

I offered words of encouragement and love to her, and she appeared comforted.

Her comfort gave me comfort.

I felt closer to her than I have ever felt.

We seemed to be on an ethereal plane of love together.

The next day, a thought came to me.

I had missed the point all this time.

All this time, all my life, I wanted her to hear me.

That day I felt the main idea was, in fact, it was she who needed to be listened to.

She couldn't hear because she had not been heard.

In love, she had lifted the pain of me not being heard by

her.

In love, also, she lifted any responsibility for me listening to her.

The slate was clean.

Everything reduced down to pure love.

Everything awash in my mother's eternal love for me.

And So It Is.

END NOTES

[1] Schwartz, Arthur, Fred Astaire, Nanette Fabray, Adolph Deutsch, Jack Buchanan, and India Adams, writers. *The Band Wagon: Selections from M-G-M Technicolor Film*. MGM, 1953.

Made in the USA
Las Vegas, NV
04 May 2021

22496238R00069